Craft Business

Ultimate Strategies For Selling Crafts and Handmade Items Online

RAYMOND WEIDLEMAN

© Copyright 2018 - All rights reserved.

In no way is it legal to reproduce, duplicate, or transmit any part of this document by either electronic means or in printed format. Recording of this publication is strictly prohibited, and any storage of this document is not allowed without written permission from the publisher.

This publication is geared towards providing exact and reliable information in regard to the topics and issues covered. The publication is not a substitute for legal, tax, financial or professional advice. If such advice is necessary, a practiced individual in the profession should be consulted.

The publisher makes no guarantees regarding income as a result of applying the information contained in this document, and any liability regarding inattention or otherwise, by any usage or abuse of any policies, processes, or directions contained within is the solitary and utter responsibility of the recipient reader, and as such, for all intents and purposes, this document is to be considered as being "for entertainment purposes only." The reader should always seek the advice of a professional when making any legal, tax, financial, or business decisions.

Under no circumstances will any legal responsibility or blame be held against the publisher for any reparation, damages, or monetary loss due to the information herein, either directly or indirectly.

Any trademarks or brands mentioned in this publication are without any consent, permission, or backing of the trademark owner.

All trademarks and brands within this book are used only for the purposes of clarification, and are owned by the owners themselves, and not affiliated with this publication.

All copyrights not held by the publisher are owned by the respective authors.

Introduction

As of March 4, 2015, Etsy, the online crafts marketplace had a whopping 54 million members and an estimated annual sales revenue of $1.95+ billion. Compared to the ever-burgeoning online retail marketplace that stood at around $300 billion in 2014, for a marketplace that's barely 10 years old, and a marketplace that deals in crafts, vintage, and unique factory items, Etsy is doing extremely well.

What makes Etsy unique from other online marketplaces such as eBay and Amazon is its flair for handmade items, crafts, vintage items, and unique factory items. If we compare Etsy's popularity to the total crafts market, estimated at around 30 billion dollars, we can conclude that Etsy is the best marketplace for any crafts merchant. Hence, this book focuses on running a craft business utilizing the power of Etsy.

Etsy is doing so well that thousands of people across the globe are creating crafts, listing them on Etsy, creating a community around their items, and selling their crafts on the platform with some making enough money to replace their day jobs and sell crafts full-time on Etsy.

Like everything else, becoming a top rated seller on Etsy is no easy task. It takes a lot of dedication, passion, patience, innovation and most importantly, a success strategy. The unfortunate news is that successfully selling crafts on Etsy requires different strategies. This can be a bit daunting for someone with no prior Etsy selling experience, but it doesn't have to be.

This book will outline all the latest strategies you need to turn your love for crafts, and your Etsy store into a thriving business.

Let's start with the most basic strategy.

Table of Contents

Introduction	4
Getting Started	7
Gearing Up For Success	12
Knocking On Success Doors	16
Smart Etsy Craft Marketing Strategies And Creative Strategies For More Sales	22
Creative Strategies For More Etsy Sales	25
Conclusion	27

Getting Started: Deciding What To Sell On Etsy- The Ultimate Strategy

As we have highlighted, success on Etsy does not come easy. It depends on how well the different strategies you implement work towards bringing you the Etsy success you yearn and long for as an artisan or crafts seller.

Etsy is a competitive marketplace. Although this is good news on one end, it is also bad news on the other end. The bad news in that as in every other marketplace, not every item listed on Etsy is a sure winner. Don't let this scare you though.

If you are like most artisans, you're probably very artistic. Although this is good news, it also makes it relatively difficult for you to decide on one area of specialty. For example, how do you know if you should sell handmade jewelry, handmade clothes, unique items, etc.?

Unfortunately, this question weighs heavy on every Etsy seller before he or she opens his or her Etsy store. Moreover, since every artisan is different, there are no industry standard guidelines aimed at helping Etsy sellers decide what to sell.

Regardless, you need to analyze things strategically before making any rash decisions about what you're going to sell on Etsy. Thus, developing a crafts selling strategy is an important part of your Etsy success. What is a crafts selling strategy?

A crafts selling strategy is basically the strategy through which you decide what to sell on Etsy. To create your Etsy crafts selling strategy, ask yourself the following five questions:

1. Why do you want to sell on Etsy?
2. What is your major driving factor?
3. Are you in this solely for the money or is your desire to build a brand around your crafts?
4. Are you passionate about something that can be considered a craft?
5. Where do you see your Etsy crafts store in the next 2 to 5 years?

Most sellers on Etsy start their Etsy store for different reasons or purposes. For example, while Etsy lists handmade items, if you visit the Etsy forums, you will realize that there are dozens of vintage item collectors successfully running Etsy stores dedicated to vintage items.

To decide what you should be selling on Etsy, you need to consider the following:

Consider Your Crafts And Relate Them To The 5 Characteristics Of Good Etsy Products

Etsy is a crafts marketplace.

Crafts can basically be considered as being art. And as we all know, or all should know, the value of art is very much relative. That is why despite being a crafts marketplace;

unique items such as cereal spoons also make Etsy's best sellers list.

You could be great at crocheting. Or you could be great at producing handmade jewelry or glass. Or you could have no special skills, but have a certain creative spark and artistic flair which allows you to create things which satisfy a certain market, like creating personalized garden signs.

To determine your passion, get out a pen and paper, and write a list of all the different types of crafts that you can create, or all the unique store items you are passionate about and that you can sell on Etsy. Here is my sample list:

1. Custom made spectacle frames
2. Custom made wedding handkerchiefs
3. Custom made leather bracelets
4. Handmade jewelry
5. Handmade fitted suits for men
6. Handmade beaded women's sandals
7. Vintage old mid-16th-century art

Create a rough list of items you would possibly put in your store. You do not have to create the list in one day. Take your time; and perhaps even ask for some ideas from your friends and family. If there is something your friends have said you're good at, then think about what you can create with that skill. For example, if you're good at making bracelets, then you can explore that avenue.

After you create your list, take a look at the following essentials of a good Etsy product in order to help you to narrow down which products you should actually decide to sell.

The 5 Essentials Of A Good Etsy Product

What makes an Etsy product good is its uniqueness. However, there are certain other characteristics that denote a classic winner on Etsy. Here they are:

1. Small, easy to pick up, and ship. Bigger items tend not to do so well on Etsy (most best-selling Etsy stores sell small items that are easy to ship and handle). Think of it in this manner: bigger items are going to cost more to ship and are more difficult to handle. If your items are too big, shipping them out could pose a problem.

2. Awesome products target a specific market or niche. It is relatively difficult to do well with your Etsy store if you fail to target a specific market demographic. For example, if you opt to go with a generic necklace, you may end up disappointed. However, by defining your target market, you can then define your product. For example, instead of 'handmade jewelry', I would drill down on the necklace niche to come up with something a bit more unique and specific. For example, I could do 'handmade bridal glass and bead jewelry'. This not only makes it easier to zero in on your craft, it also makes it easier to customize your marketing approach for your desired target audience.

3. Good crafts often cost between $10 to $250. If you visit the Etsy best-sellers list you will quickly notice that most of the items listed there retail somewhere between $10 to $250. This in no way means that there is less money to be made in products above this price range. What it means is that most Etsy buyers are most likely to buy items in that price range.

4. Good products are popular. Popularity in this case means that good products have a steady stream of buyers throughout the year.

5. Profitable items sell for twice as much as their cost of production or buying price. Etsy is all about helping your craft business grow and expand. The growth of your Etsy store means the growth of your craft business. You cannot grow your store if it is not profitable. When pricing your items, always consider the total cost of production and aim to price your crafts at least twice as high as the initial production or buying price. Aim for nothing less than a 50% profit margin.

Now that we have outlined a strategy you can follow to choose a profitable craft you can list on Etsy, you'll hopefully be able to decide on one.

The remainder of this book will be dedicated to outlining the different strategies you'll need in order to make your craft business profitable.

Gearing Up For Success: Smart Strategies For Setting Up A Successful Etsy Shop

Now that you have decided on an item or items to sell on Etsy, you are ready to get started selling on Etsy.

Signing up for an Etsy account is easy. All you need to do is navigate to the Etsy Homepage (www.etsy.com), register an account, verify your email and voila! You're done!

The name you choose for your store and how you brand it plays a very important role in the profitability of your Etsy shop. Therefore, let's look at different strategies you can employ to ensure that your Etsy shop starts off on the right foot.

Strategy 1: Identify Your Target Market And Brand Your Shop Around Their Wants And Needs

Before you create your Etsy store and start listing your crafts, a very important area to consider is that of identifying your ideal customer.

To whom do the crafts appeal to? Whom do you intend to sell to? What is the persona of your ideal customer? Are you targeting a younger demographic or an older one, are you targeting business travelers or busy stay at home moms? What are their characteristics? What is their income level?

It is very important that you form a very clear picture of your ideal customer and understand their needs.

This step may seem irrelevant in a broader sense, but it's a crucial step, one you must undertake and one that will define how you conduct your business.

Strategy 2: Create Your Brand Around Your Target Market

Different demographics and genders respond differently to different things. Thus, you want to think about what makes your brand appealing to your target market, and not to any other kind of market.

When creating a brand that appeals to your target market, it is crucial to pay proper attention to how you name your store. It is important to make the name something catchy and something your Etsy buyers can relate to your crafts.

Note: It is totally okay to use your name as your Etsy store's name, especially if your crafts are already a recognizable brand. At the same time, you should aim to create a unique brand that speaks volumes about your tastes as well as speaks volumes for your crafts.

Creating a brand is not just about the name. It also includes paying attention to the visual aesthetics of your store as well as the style in which product photos are taken and product descriptions are written.

Also, you want to use the 'about page' to tell your unique story, which is also part of your brand. Many people will make a buying decision based off of your 'about page', so the more interesting you make it the better.

Also note, that creating a brand is not a one-time thing; it is something most companies develop and improve upon over time.

Strategy 3: Spy On Your Competition

Unless you have invented a new craft, it is highly unlikely that your craft will be the only one of its kind on the Etsy marketplace. Moreover, if your craft is the only one of its kind on the entire Etsy store, it is highly unlikely that it has a ready market (which is one of the key characteristics of a good Etsy product).

Strategy 4: Fill Out Your Account Information Correctly

If all the information in your Etsy account is not complete, you are shooting yourself in the foot. Filling out all the information on your account means:

Creating a unique banner

Now that your shop is up, the next step is to create a banner for your shop. A banner for your shop is fundamental because it is, in fact, the first thing all prospective buyers will notice about you. A standard banner on Etsy is about 100 pixels high, 760 pixels wide, and a web standard resolution (72 DPI).

Choosing an avatar

If you are serious about making money on Etsy, your profile must not lack an avatar. Think of an avatar as a logo for your business. Make your avatar distinctive and eye-catching. But do not shy away from using your picture as this has been shown to increase buyer trust.

Completing your profile

Regardless of what you intend to sell; your profile must be the envy of other sellers. Your profile is your most important selling point. It tells your prospective buyers who you are, why your items are worth purchasing, and how you run your store.

The opening paragraph on your profile must make the eyes of the buyer gleam with excitement. The paragraphs that follow should also follow this logic. Think of your profile as a chance to tell your story. Make it extremely friendly so it portrays the image of an approachable retailer. I have found that while most sellers try to outdo each other with their creative storytelling, they forget to include just enough personal information to make the store personal and not too professional. It is also important to make sure that your store adheres to Etsy's general store policies.

Next, we shall look at how to list items to make them stand out in the marketplace.

Knocking On Success Doors: Etsy's Product Listing Strategies That Work

Now that you have settled on a craft to list on Etsy, created a store, and branded it, it is about time we got started with listing our products on the Etsy marketplace.

While it may be easy, and seem irrelevant, how you create your listing on Etsy determines if you make any sales. Although each seller has a different approach to creating listings, there is an industry standard model of listing products that when infused with your uniqueness (brand and crafts) will increase your chances of making sales.

Let us look at these industry standards guaranteed to attract sales to your listings.

Step 1: Create compelling titles

When creating your Etsy crafts titles, imagine you're creating a newspaper headline. What is synonymous with all newspaper headlines? Newspaper titles grab attention.

You want your Etsy product titles to follow the same concept. You should aim to create great crafts titles that compel Etsy buyers to click on them. Creating great titles is not as hard as you may have thought. To create great titles, do the following:

1. Create brief titles- Etsy offers you about 140 characters as your product title description. Aim to keep your titles brief. However, they should not be so brief as to compromise on the product's appeal. Your

job as an Etsy seller is to create short compelling product titles that compel readers to click on them.

2. Include the name of the product on the title- When a buyer goes into Etsy looking for a specific item, they use this item name in their search. For example, if someone searches for handmade unique bracelets, they use the term bracelet in their search. This way, that individual is sure that the resulting search results relate to their initial search. Ensure that no matter how short and succinct your title is, it features the name of the product you're listing. Moreover, because Etsy search is similar to the Google search engine in that it specifically lists items related to user searches, make a point of employing target specific keywords in your titles.

3. Don't use all caps- There is a misconception that writing titles in all caps attracts more attention. This is a fallacy. When you write titles or anything else for that matter in caps, it indicates that you're putting off your customers because most people construe the meaning of ALL CAPS to mean you are yelling. It is never a wise choice to yell at your potential customers. Instead of capitalizing everything, use title case and capitalize the first letter of each word. Doing this will serve a better purpose than if you had used all caps.

Step 2: Pictures are your bread and butter

When Etsy buyers visit your store and view your listing, even though you hold the physical product, what you're selling to the buyer is a picture of the end product that you'll ship to him or her. Therefore, your crafts listing should feature the most compelling pictures you can manage. This does in no way mean that you should be a professional photographer or hire one (you may have to hire one if you don't own quality equipment that can capture captivating images). All it means is that you have to become a perfectionist who pays attention to details. To take compelling images, adhere to the following:

1. Avoid photos taken from a distance- When you take up-close photos, the items you are taking shots of fill the frame. The closer the item is, the higher the chances that the item will be more visible and appealing to the customers. Moreover, slight-angled shots are better at giving your items more depth compared to front facing direct shots.

2. If your camera supports it, blur your photo background to ensure that the end image focuses on the product. This ensures that the customers' eyes are transfixed on the listed item rather than some awesome looking painting in the background.

3. Do not include multiple items in your shots- Unless you're selling related items, ensure that all your pictures feature one item and one item only. Using multi-item pictures on your listings will only confuse potential customers.

4. If your craft offering is available in different colors, include eye-catching and alluring photos of the item in different colors, (and styles if you offer different styles).

5. Use good lighting- Customers should not squint in order to decipher your listing images. Use good natural lighting where possible to ensure that your images appear clear and not blurry. Moreover, you should take several shots of the same item from different angles.

Step 3: Create detailed and honest listing descriptions

Once you have created your item title, taken compelling pictures and uploaded them to the listing page (ideally, you want to have your pictures ready before you start listing your crafts), the final bit of creating your listings is by creating a product description.

As a crafter or craft lover yourself, how would it feel if you bought a craft that upon opening did not match the described item? My guess is you would be very angry.

Do not be deceitful in your craft item details. Remember this: your description is your final pitch to the customer. Most online buyers will make a purchase depending on the item description.

Create detailed item-descriptions that clearly describes the item as it is. Include critical information such as size, material, and all other details relevant to the craft you're listing. For example, if an item is breakable, state that in the item description. If it is pet-friendly, state that to sway pet owners.

Coincidentally, creating compelling but truthful craft item descriptions is one of the best ways to keep your return rate low. Moreover, because Etsy is a search engine, optimizing your item title and description is also one of the best ways to appear in internal Etsy searches and external Google and other search engine searches.

Like the product titles, your description should also not be overly long. It should be thorough, short, sweet, and keyword optimized for search (in terms of keyword optimization, it is important to note that even though creating keyword optimized item titles and descriptions is beneficial, using keywords on your listings should not compromise human readability).

On listing your crafts on Etsy, aim to ensure that your titles are catchy and compelling to buyers. After creating compelling titles, when customers click on the compelling titles and images, use the item description page to get your customers excited about owning your items.

Step 4: Be succinct about shipping

After wooing in your target audience with enticing pictures and an alluring title, after using the item description part of your listing to get the almost buyer excited about your craft, to make a sale and convert that potential customer into a buyer, you should aim to have a very detailed and thorough shipping and returns policy.

Online buyers want to have their item as fast as possible after paying for it. Clearly define when the item ships after someone makes a purchase. Other than wanting their online purchase as fast as possible, online buyers also want to know that if an item does not meet their expectations (within reason of course), they can ship it back for a refund or another item. Aim to have a clear return policy that outlines conditions of return, return shipping costs, and all other important shipping-related details. Also, provide a medium through which your customers can easily reach you through in case of returns or problems with shipping.

If you were following through these steps by creating your own listing, you should now have a fully branded store with at least one optimized crafts listing. Now, if you had drilled down on your craft and chosen your item using the 5 key characteristics of a good item, your item has a ready market. However, because your store is new at this particular moment, work on listing a few more items (aim for about 10 to 20 optimized items).

Although different, owning an Etsy store is no different from owning or running any other business. In case you missed business 101, business 101 states the following: *if you fail to advertise your business, you are planning to fail.* To scale up your Etsy business, you need to ensure that your listings are visible to the right people and are reaching the right customers.

In the next chapter, we shall look at different Etsy marketing strategies and touch on creative strategies aimed at increasing your sales.

Smart Etsy Craft Marketing Strategies And Creative Strategies For More Sales

Other than creating awesome crafts oozing personality, charm, and uniqueness, the other very important thing you have to consider is how to market your Etsy store and crafts.

Most successful Etsy sellers will be quick to point out that they spend more than a third of their time on marketing their Etsy stores and products. Marketing in this case is relative. It could mean creating search engine optimized listings that appear first on internal and external searches for specific keywords and related keywords, or it could mean participating in blogs relevant to your target audience.

Regardless of how you do it, you cannot overlook the importance of marketing your Etsy store and crafts. Creating an effective Etsy crafts marketing strategy can sometimes be intimidating. It does not have to be. To create your marketing strategy, follow the following tips:

Step 1: Show your store some love

Etsy is a unique marketplace and although most of the items listed are beautiful in their own right, what appeals to most buyers is the story behind the craft. In fact, most Etsy buyers will buy from you because they can relate to the story you tell.

There is no better place to let your unique story shine through than by using the about page. Ensure that you have a profile avatar that tells a story. A banner that tells your store's story all wrapped up with a nice description of yourself, your craft, and everything else that makes you and your craft unique. Ensure that your about page, store banner, and item description all let the uniqueness of your crafts and store shine through.

Step 2: SEO is central to marketing

80% of all online transactions start at the search bar. The same applies to Etsy sales. Most Etsy buyers use keywords to search for the product they want. For example, someone might navigate to the Etsy search bar and type 'handmade jewelry'. This will prompt Etsy to list all listings relevant to the specific search.

To optimize the chance of buyers finding your listings, be sure to optimize your descriptions and titles. Ensure that these two key areas have keywords relevant to the buyers. The key to nailing this is asking yourself the following question: what terms does my target audience use when searching for crafts related to mine?

SEO plays a very critical part in the success of your store. Unfortunately, most sellers optimize their stores hoping to draw sales the very next day. SEO is not aspirin. Even though the SEO you perform on your store starts to work today, it will not immediately reflect on your balance sheet. Additionally, developing the right keywords and SEO strategy for your store takes practice, patience, and experimentation.

Step 3: Go social

A huge percentage of Etsy buyers are social media users (Facebook to be precise). If you're serious about marketing your brand, crafts and Etsy shop, you should have a presence on social media. If your target audience is active on Facebook or Twitter, engage them and market to them. If your target is active on certain forums and blogs, become an active participant and contributor to these blogs and forums. When you add value to your target market's lives and when your target audience can recognize your name, it is easier for them to trust you and make purchases from you.

Creative Strategies For More Etsy Sales

First things first: to generate a ton of sales for your Etsy store and crafts, you have to treat your Etsy store as you would treat any other business. This may mean setting goals. Create goals for your Etsy business. For example, to increase your sales, think of the number you aim to generate within a specific timeline and follow these strategies.

Step 1: Go listing crazy

If your store is new, before you use the marketing strategies we outlined earlier, ensure you have at least 10 listings on your store. More listings increase your chances of being found by shoppers. More people discovering your crafts translate into more potential buyers and potential sales.

Regardless of the age status of your store (new or old), create a posting schedule. Ensure that all your listings are search optimized. Focus on consistently listing new crafts in your store (add about 10 to 15 new items each week. Note that renewing sold items also count as new listings). If 10 to 15 listing seem too many, and you can't create that many products, you can create different variations of your item (maybe an item in a different color) and list that separately.

Step 2: Pay attention to your money shots

A picture is worth a thousand words. Earlier on, we mentioned that even though you are selling physical products, your potential customers' first brush with your craft offering is through the pictures on your listing. In the online marketplace, clear, high-quality pictures are a crucial selling point. Ensure that your craft photography is clear high definition.

Step 3: Set up international shipping

Today, the world is a global marketplace. Do not restrict your shop's profitability by failing to sell to the global market. Allowing for international shipping will ensure that your crafts reach a bigger market. A bigger market is equal to more sales.

Step 4: Track your progress

You can use your shop stats to determine if your marketing strategy is working. The shop stats give you a complete snapshot of how many people are viewing your listing, your orders, and revenues.

Conclusion

It is truly possible to sell on Etsy and make profits. However, you have to make deliberate efforts towards discovering what works and what does not work if you are to truly make profits and keep on getting more. As a rule of thumb, you must treat your Etsy business like any other business if you really want to go on to make big money in the process.